# David Buys a Dog

by Susan Jones Leeming
illustrated by Chi Chung

PEARSON
Scott
Foresman

Editorial Offices: Glenview, Illinois • Parsippany, New Jersey • New York, New York
Sales Offices: Needham, Massachusetts • Duluth, Georgia • Glenview, Illinois
Coppell, Texas • Ontario, California • Mesa, Arizona

Every effort has been made to secure permission and provide appropriate credit for photographic material. The publisher deeply regrets any omission and pledges to correct errors called to its attention in subsequent editions.

Unless otherwise acknowledged, all photographs are the property of Scott Foresman, a division of Pearson Education.

Photo locators denoted as follows: Top (T), Center (C), Bottom (B), Left (L), Right (R), Background (Bkgd)

Illustrations by Chi Chung

Photograph 12 Comstock Royalty Free

ISBN: 0-328-13331-0

7 8 9 10  V0G1  14 13 12 11 10 09 08

Every morning Davis greeted his dog
friends. All day long Davis thought about
dogs. Every night Davis read about dogs.
Davis dreamed of dogs every night too.
Davis wanted a dog of his own.

"I want a dog of my own," said Davis.

"Dogs are expensive," Dad said.

"Will a dog cost a thousand dollars?" asked Davis.

"No. You'll need about seventy dollars," Dad said. "How much have you saved?"

Davis stacked his ten quarters, seven dimes, eleven nickels, and thirty-seven pennies. He added the stacks to find the value. "That's $2.50 worth of quarters, plus 70¢ in dimes, plus 55¢ in nickels, plus 37¢ in pennies. I have $4.12," Davis said.

Davis knew that $4.12 was not enough money to buy a dog. He would have to earn more. *I need to get a job,* he thought.

Davis saw a sign on his way home from school. The corner store needed someone to deliver newspapers on Saturdays. *I can do that!* Davis thought.

"Mom! I can deliver newspapers to earn money!" Davis shouted. "Now I can get a dog of my own!"

So Davis delivered newspapers on Saturdays. Mom followed on her bicycle.

Every week the man at the store gave Davis a check. Davis put the checks in a savings account at the bank. Every month the money in the bank earned interest. The amount in Davis's account grew.

On the fifth Saturday, Davis and Mom visited the pet store. Davis bought a collar and leash for his dog. Davis wished he had a million dollars to spend. He wanted to buy every dog toy!

Soon Davis had enough money to buy his dog. Buddy, a furry brown and white puppy, came to live with Davis, Mom, and Dad. At last Davis had a dog of his own!

# Economics

Economics is the study of how people make and use goods and services. Economists, the people who study economics, look at trends or patterns in how people earn, save, and spend money. Using this information, economists try to predict how people, companies, and countries will earn, save, and spend money in the future.